ERNEST FENOLLOSA

*The chinese written character
as a medium for poetry*

EDITED BY

EZRA POUND

CITY LIGHTS BOOKS
SAN FRANCISCO

© 1936 by Ezra Pound
First City Lights edition 1968

Cover design by John Miller / Black and White Design

Tenth printing: February 1991

ISBN 0-87286-014-0
LC Catalog Card Number 64-11470

City Lights Books are available to bookstores through our primary distributor:
Subterranean Company. P. O. Box 168, 265 S. 5th St., Monroe, OR 97456.
Tel. 1-503-847-5274. Toll-free orders 1-800-274-7826. FAX 503-847-6018.
Our books are also available through library jobbers and regional distributors.
For personal orders and catalogs, please write to City Lights Books,
261 Columbus Avenue, San Francisco CA 94133.

CITY LIGHTS BOOKS are edited by Lawrence Ferlinghetti
and Nancy J. Peters and published at the City Lights Bookstore,
261 Columbus Avenue, San Francisco, California 94133.

THE CHINESE WRITTEN CHARACTER
AS A MEDIUM FOR POETRY

[*This essay was practically finished by the late Ernest Fenollosa; I have done little more than remove a few repetitions and shape a few sentences.*

We have here not a bare philological discussion, but a study of the fundamentals of all aesthetics. In his search through unknown art Fenollosa, coming upon unknown motives and principles unrecognised in the West, was already led into many modes of thought since fruitful in ' new ' Western painting and poetry. He was a forerunner without knowing it and without being known as such.

He discerned principles of writing which he had scarcely time to put into practice. In Japan he restored, or greatly helped to restore, a respect for the native art. In America and Europe he cannot be looked upon as a mere searcher after exotics. His mind was constantly filled with parallels and comparisons between Eastern and Western art. To him the exotic was always a means of fructification. He looked to an American renaissance. The vitality of his outlook can be judged from the fact that although this essay was written some time before his death in 1908 I have not had to change the allusions to Western conditions. The later movements in art have corroborated his theories. E.P. 1918.]

This twentieth century not only turns a new page in the book of the world, but opens another and a startling chapter. Vistas of strange futures unfold for man, of world-embracing cultures half-weaned from Europe, of hitherto undreamed responsibilities for nations and races.

The Chinese problem alone is so vast that no nation can afford to ignore it. We in America, especially, must face it across the Pacific, and master it or it will master us. And the only way to master it is to strive with patient sympathy to understand the best, the most hopeful and the most human elements in it.

It is unfortunate that England and America have so long ignored or mistaken the deeper problems of Oriental culture. We have misconceived the Chinese for a materialistic people, for a debased and worn-out race. We have belittled the Japanese as a nation of copyists. We have stupidly assumed that Chinese history affords no glimpse of change in social evolution, no salient epoch of moral and spiritual crisis. We have denied the essential humanity of these peoples; and we have toyed with their ideals as if they were no better than comic songs in an ' opéra bouffe.'

The duty that faces us is not to batter down their forts or to exploit their markets, but to study and to come to sympathize with their humanity and their generous aspirations. Their type of cultivation has been high. Their harvest of recorded experience doubles our own. The Chinese have been idealists, and experimenters in the making of great principles; their history opens a world of lofty aim and achievement, parallel to that of the ancient Mediterranean peoples. We need their best ideals to supplement our own — ideals enshrined in their art, in their literature and in the tragedies of their lives.

We have already seen proof of the vitality and practical value of Oriental painting for ourselves and as a key to the Eastern soul. It may be worth while to approach their literature, the intensest part of it, their poetry, even in an imperfect manner.

I feel that I should perhaps apologize* for presuming to

*[The apology was unnecessary, but Professor Fenollosa saw fit to make it, and I therefore transcribe his words. E.P.]

follow that series of brilliant scholars, Davis, Legge, St. Denys and Giles, who have treated the subject of Chinese poetry with a wealth of erudition to which I can proffer no claim. It is not as a professional linguist nor as a sinologue that I humbly put forward what I have to say. As an enthusiastic student of beauty in Oriental culture, having spent a large portion of my years in close relation with Orientals, I could not but breathe in something of the poetry incarnated in their lives.

I have been for the most part moved to my temerity by personal considerations. An unfortunate belief has spread both in England and in America that Chinese and Japanese poetry are hardly more than an amusement, trivial, childish, and not to be reckoned in the world's serious literary performance. I have heard well-known sinologues state that, save for the purposes of professional linguistic scholarship, these branches of poetry are fields too barren to repay the toil necessary for their cultivation.

Now my own impression has been so radically and diametrically opposed to such a conclusion, that a sheer enthusiasm of generosity has driven me to wish to share with other Occidentals my newly discovered joy. Either I am pleasingly self-deceived in my positive delight, or else there must be some lack of aesthetic sympathy and of poetic feeling in the accepted methods of presenting the poetry of China. I submit my causes of joy.

Failure or success in presenting any alien poetry in English must depend largely upon poetic workmanship in the chosen medium. It was perhaps too much to expect that aged scholars who had spent their youth in gladiatorial combats with the refractory Chinese characters should succeed also as poets. Even Greek verse might have fared equally ill had its purveyors been perforce content with provincial standards of English rhyming. Sinologues should remember that the purpose of poetical translation is the poetry, not the verbal definitions in dictionaries.

One modest merit I may, perhaps, claim for my work : it represents for the first time a Japanese school of study in Chinese culture. Hitherto Europeans have been somewhat at the mercy of contemporary Chinese scholarship. Several centuries ago China lost much of her creative self, and of her insight into the causes of her own life; but her original spirit still lives, grows, interprets, transferred to Japan in all its original freshness. The Japanese today represent a stage of culture roughly corresponding to that of China under the Sung dynasty. I have been fortunate in studying for many years as a private pupil under Professor Kainan Mori, who is probably the greatest living authority on Chinese poetry. He has recently been called to a chair in the Imperial University of Tokio.

My subject is poetry, not language, yet the roots of poetry are in language. In the study of a language so alien in form to ours as is Chinese in its written character, it is necessary to inquire how these universal elements of form which constitute poetics can derive appropriate nutriment.

In what sense can verse, written in terms of visible hieroglyphics, be reckoned true poetry? It might seem that poetry, which like music is a *time art,* weaving its unities out of successive impressions of sound, could with difficulty assimilate a verbal medium consisting largely of semipictorial appeals to the eye.

Contrast, for example, Gray's line :

> *The curfew tolls the knell of parting day*

with the Chinese line :

月　耀　如　晴　雪

Moon　　*Rays*　　*Like*　　*Pure*　　*Snow*

Unless the sound of the latter be given, what have they in common? It is not enough to adduce that each contains a certain body of prosaic meaning; for the question is, how can the Chinese line imply, *as form,* the very element that distinguishes poetry from prose?

On second glance, it is seen that the Chinese words, though visible, occur in just as necessary an order as the phonetic symbols of Gray. All that poetic form requires is a regular and flexible sequence, as plastic as thought itself. The characters may be seen and read, silently by the eye, one after the other :

Moon rays like pure snow.

Perhaps we do not always sufficiently consider that thought is successive, not through some accident or weakness of our subjective operations but because the operations of nature are successive. The transferences of force from agent to object, which constitute natural phenomena, occupy time. Therefore, a reproduction of them in imagination requires the same temporal order.*

Suppose that we look out of a window and watch a man. Suddenly he turns his head and actively fixes his attention upon something. We look ourselves and see that his vision has been focused upon a horse. We saw, first, the man before he acted; second, while he acted; third, the object

---

*[Style, that is to say, limpidity, as opposed to rhetoric. E.P.]

toward which his action was directed. In speech we split up the rapid continuity of this action and of its picture into its three essential parts or joints in the right order, and say :

Man sees horse.

It is clear that these three joints, or words, are only three phonetic symbols, which stand for the three terms of a natural process. But we could quite as easily denote these three stages of our thought by symbols equally arbitrary, *which had no basis in sound;* for example, by three Chinese characters :

Man   Sees   Horse

If we all knew *what division* of this mental horse-picture each of these signs stood for, we could communicate continuous thought to one another as easily by drawing them as by speaking words. We habitually employ the visible language of gesture in much this same manner.

But Chinese notation is something much more than arbitrary symbols. It is based upon a vivid shorthand picture of the operations of nature. In the algebraic figure and in the spoken word there is no natural connection between thing and sign : all depends upon sheer convention. But the Chinese method follows natural suggestion. First stands the man on his two legs. Second, his eye moves through space : a bold figure represented by running legs under an eye, a modified picture of an eye, a modified picture of running legs, but unforgettable once you have seen it. Third stands the horse on his four legs.

The thought-picture is not only called up by these signs

as well as by words, but far more vividly and concretely. Legs belong to all three characters : they are *alive*. The group holds something of the quality of a continuous moving picture.

The untruth of a painting or a photograph is that, in spite of its concreteness, it drops the element of natural succession.

Contrast the Laocoön statue with Browning's lines :
> ' *I sprang to the stirrup, and Joris, and he*
>
> . . . . . .
>
> *And into the midnight we galloped abreast.*'

One superiority of verbal poetry as an art rests in its getting back to the fundamental reality of *time*. Chinese poetry has the unique advantage of combining both elements. It speaks at once with the vividness of painting, and with the mobility of sounds. It is, in some sense, more objective than either, more dramatic. In reading Chinese we do not seem to be juggling mental counters, but to be watching *things* work out their own fate.

Leaving for a moment the form of the sentence, let us look more closely at this quality of vividness in the structure of detached Chinese words. The earlier forms of these characters were pictorial, and their hold upon the imagination is little shaken, even in later conventional modifications. It is not so well known, perhaps, that the great number of these ideographic roots carry in them a *verbal idea of action*. It might be thought that a picture is naturally the picture of a *thing*, and that therefore the root ideas of Chinese are what grammar calls nouns.

But examination shows that a large number of the primitive Chinese characters, even the so-called radicals, are shorthand pictures of actions or processes.

For example, the ideograph meaning ' to speak ' is a

mouth with two words and a flame coming out of it. The sign meaning 'to grow up with difficulty' is grass with a twisted root (*vide* Plates 2 and 4). But this concrete *verb* quality, both in nature and in the Chinese signs, becomes far more striking and poetic when we pass from such simple, original pictures to compounds. In this process of compounding, two things added together do not produce a third thing but suggest some fundamental relation between them. For example, the ideograph for a 'messmate' is a man and a fire (*vide* Plate 2, col. 2).

A true noun, an isolated thing, does not exist in nature. Things are only the terminal points, or rather the meeting points, of actions, cross-sections cut through actions, snapshots. Neither can a pure verb, an abstract motion, be possible in nature. The eye sees noun and verb as one : things in motion, motion in things, and so the Chinese conception tends to represent them.*

The sun underlying the bursting forth of plants=spring.

The sun sign tangled in the branches of the tree sign= east (*vide* Plate 2).

'Rice-field' plus 'struggle'=male (*vide* Plate 2, col. 3).

'Boat' plus 'water'=boat-water, a ripple (*vide* Plate 2, col. 1).

Let us return to the form of the sentence and see what power it adds to the verbal units from which it builds. I wonder how many people have asked themselves why the sentence form exists at all, why it seems so universally necessary *in all languages?* Why *must* all possess it, and what is the normal type of it? If it be so universal, it ought to correspond to some primary law of nature.

I fancy the professional grammarians have given but a

*[Axe *striking* something; dog *attending* man=dogs him.]
[*Vide* Plate 2, col. 3.]

lame response to this inquiry. Their definitions fall into two types: one, that a sentence expresses a 'complete thought'; the other, that in it we bring about a union of subject and predicate.

The former has the advantage of trying for some natural objective standard, since it is evident that a thought can not be the test of its own completeness. But in nature there is *no* completeness. On the one hand, practical completeness may be expressed by a mere interjection, as ' Hi! there!', or ' Scat!', or even by shaking one's fist. No sentence is needed to make one's meaning more clear. On the other hand, no full sentence really completes a thought. The man who sees and the horse which is seen will not stand still. The man was planning a ride before he looked. The horse kicked when the man tried to catch him. The truth is that acts are successive, even continuous; one causes or passes into another. And though we may string ever so many clauses into a single compound sentence, motion leaks everywhere, like electricity from an exposed wire. All processes in nature are interrelated; and thus there could be no complete sentence (according to this definition) save one which it would take all time to pronounce.

In the second definition of the sentence, as 'uniting a subject and a predicate,' the grammarian falls back on pure subjectivity. *We* do it all; it is a little private juggling between our right and left hands. The subject is that about which *I* am going to talk; the predicate is that which *I* am going to say about it. The sentence according to this definition is not an attribute of nature but an accident of man as a conversational animal.

If it were really so, then there could be no possible test of the truth of a sentence. Falsehood would be as specious as verity. Speech would carry no conviction.

Of course this view of the grammarians springs from the discredited, or rather the useless, logic of the Middle Ages. According to this logic, thought deals with abstractions, concepts drawn out of things by a sifting process. These logicians never inquired how the ' qualities ' which they pulled out of things came to be there. The truth of all their little checker-board juggling depended upon the natural order by which these powers or properties or qualities were folded in concrete things, yet they despised the ' thing ' as a mere ' particular,' or pawn. It was as if Botany should reason from the leaf-patterns woven into our table-cloths. Valid scientific thought consists in following as closely as may be the actual and entangled lines of forces as they pulse through things. Thought deals with no bloodless concepts but watches *things move* under its microscope.

The sentence form was forced upon primitive men by nature itself. It was not we who made it; it was a reflection of the temporal order in causation. All truth has to be expressed in sentences because all truth is the *transference of power*. The type of sentence in nature is a flash of lightning. It passes between two terms, a cloud and the earth. No unit of natural process can be less than this. All natural processes are, in their units, as much as this. Light, heat, gravity, chemical affinity, human will, have this in common, that they redistribute force. Their unit of process can be represented as :

term	*transference*	*term*
from	*of*	*to*
which	*force*	*which*

If we regard this transference as the conscious or unconscious act of an agent we can translate the diagram into :

agent	*act*	*object*

In this the act is the very substance of the fact denoted. The agent and the object are only limiting terms.

It seems to me that the normal and typical sentence in English as well as in Chinese expresses just this unit of natural process. It consists of three necessary words : the first denoting the agent or subject from which the act starts, the second embodying the very stroke of the act, the third pointing to the object, the receiver of the impact. Thus :

Farmer   pounds   rice

The form of the Chinese transitive sentence, and of the English (omitting particles), exactly corresponds to this universal form of action in nature. This brings language close to *things,* and in its strong reliance upon verbs it erects all speech into a kind of dramatic poetry.

A different sentence order is frequent in inflected languages like Latin, German or Japanese. This is because they are inflected, i.e. they have little tags and word-endings, or labels, to show which is the agent, the object, etc. In uninflected languages, like English and Chinese, there is nothing but the order of the words to distinguish their functions. And this order would be no sufficient indication, were it not the *natural order* — that is, the order of cause and effect.

It is true that there are, in language, intransitive and passive forms, sentences built out of the verb ' to be,' and, finally, negative forms. To grammarians and logicians these have seemed more primitive than the transitive, or at least exceptions to the transitive. I had long suspected that these apparently exceptional forms had grown from the transitive or worn away from it by alteration, or modification. This view is confirmed by Chinese examples, wherein it is still possible to watch the transformation going on.

The intransitive form derives from the transitive by dropping a generalised, customary, reflexive or cognate object : ' He runs (a race).' ' The sky reddens (itself).' ' We breathe (air).' Thus we get weak and incomplete sentences which suspend the picture and lead us to think of some verbs as denoting states rather than acts. Outside grammar the word ' state ' would hardly be recognised as scientific. Who can doubt that when we say ' The wall shines,' we mean that it actively reflects light to our eye?

The beauty of Chinese verbs is that they are all transitive or intransitive at pleasure. There is no such thing as a naturally intransitive verb. The passive form is evidently a correlative sentence, which turns about and makes the object into a subject. That the object is not in itself passive, but contributes some positive force of its own to the action, is in harmony both with scientific law and with ordinary experience. The English passive voice with ' is ' seemed at first an obstacle to this hypothesis, but one suspected that the true form was a generalised transitive verb meaning something like ' receive,' which had degenerated into an auxiliary. It was a delight to find this the case in Chinese.

In nature there are no negations, no possible transfers of negative force. The presence of negative sentences in language would seem to corroborate the logicians' view that assertion is an arbitrary subjective act. *We* can assert a negation, though nature can not. But here again science comes to our aid against the logician : all apparently negative or disruptive movements bring into play other positive forces. It requires great effort to annihilate. Therefore we should suspect that, if we could follow back the history of all negative particles, we should find that they also are sprung from transitive verbs. It is too late to demonstrate such derivations in the Aryan languages, the clue has been lost; but in Chinese we can still watch positive verbal conceptions passing over into so-called negatives. Thus in Chinese the sign meaning ' to be lost in the forest ' relates to a state of non-existence. English ' not '=the Sanskrit *na,* which may come from the root *na,* to be lost, to perish.

Lastly comes the infinitive which substitutes for a specific colored verb the universal copula ' is,' followed by a noun or an adjective. We do not say a tree ' greens itself,' but ' the tree is green '; not that ' monkeys bring forth live young,' but that ' the monkey is a mammal.' This is an ultimate weakness of language. It has come from generalising all intransitive words into one. As ' live,' ' see,' ' walk,' ' breathe,' are generalised into states by dropping their objects, so these weak verbs are in turn reduced to the abstractest state of all, namely bare existence.

There is in reality no such verb as a pure copula, no such original conception; our very word *exist* means ' to stand forth,' to show oneself by a definite act. ' Is ' comes from the Aryan root *as,* to breathe. ' Be ' is from *bhu,* to grow.

In Chinese the chief verb for ' is ' not only means actively ' to have,' but shows by its derivation that it expresses something even more concrete, namely ' to snatch from the

moon with the hand."  Here the baldest symbol

of prosaic analysis is transformed by magic into a splendid flash of concrete poetry.

I shall not have entered vainly into this long analysis of the sentence if I have succeeded in showing how poetical is the Chinese form and how close to nature. In translating Chinese, verse especially, we must hold as closely as possible to the concrete force of the original, eschewing adjectives, nouns and intransitive forms wherever we can, and seeking instead strong and individual verbs.

Lastly we notice that the likeness of form between Chinese and English sentences renders translation from one to the other exceptionally easy. The genius of the two is much the same. Frequently it is possible by omitting English particles to make a literal word-for-word translation which will be not only intelligible in English, but even the strongest and most poetical English. Here, however, one must follow closely what is said, not merely what is abstractly meant.

Let us go back from the Chinese sentence to the individual written word. How are such words to be classified? Are some of them nouns by nature, some verbs and some adjectives? Are there pronouns and prepositions and conjunctions in Chinese as in good Christian languages?

One is led to suspect from an analysis of the Aryan languages that such differences are not natural, and that they have been unfortunately invented by grammarians to confuse the simple poetic outlook on life. All nations have written their strongest and most vivid literature before they invented a grammar. Moreover, all Aryan etymology points back to roots which are the equivalents of simple Sanskrit verbs, such as we find tabulated at the back of our Skeat. Nature herself has no grammar.* Fancy picking up a man and telling him that he is a noun, a dead thing rather than a bundle of functions! A ' part of speech ' is only *what it does*. Frequently our lines of cleavage fail, one part of speech

*[Even Latin, living Latin, had not the network of rules they foist upon unfortunate school-children. These are borrowed sometimes from Greek grammarians, even as I have seen English grammars borrowing oblique cases from Latin grammars. Sometimes they sprang from the grammatising or categorising passion of pedants. Living Latin had only the feel of the cases : the ablative and dative emotion. E.P.]

acts for another. They *act for* one another because they were originally one and the same.

Few of us realise that in our own language these very differences once grew up in living articulation; that they still retain life. It is only when the difficulty of placing some odd term arises, or when we are forced to translate into some very different language, that we attain for a moment the inner heat of thought, a heat which melts down the parts of speech to recast them at will.

One of the most interesting facts about the Chinese language is that in it we can see, not only the forms of sentences, but literally the parts of speech growing up, budding forth one from another. Like nature, the Chinese words are alive and plastic, because *thing* and *action* are not formally separated. The Chinese language naturally knows no grammar. It is only lately that foreigners, European and Japanese, have begun to torture this vital speech by forcing it to fit the bed of their definitions. We import into our reading of Chinese all the weakness of our own formalisms. This is especially sad in poetry, because the one necessity, even in our own poetry, is to keep words as flexible as possible, as full of the sap of nature.

Let us go further with our example. In English we call ' to shine ' a *verb in the infinitive,* because it gives the abstract meaning of the verb without conditions. If we want a corresponding adjective we take a different word, ' bright.' If we need a noun we say ' luminosity,' which is abstract, being derived from an adjective. To get a tolerably concrete noun, we have to leave behind the verb and adjective roots, and light upon a thing arbitrarily cut off from its power of action, say ' the sun ' or ' the moon.' Of course there is nothing in nature so cut off, and therefore this nounising is itself an abstraction. Even if we did have a common word underlying at once the verb 'shine,' the adjective 'bright' and the noun 'sun,' we should probably call it an 'infinitive of the infinitive.' According to our ideas, it should be something extremely abstract, too intangible for use.*

The Chinese have one word, *ming* or *mei*. Its ideograph is the sign of the sun together with the sign of the moon. It serves as verb, noun, adjective. Thus you write literally, 'the sun and moon of the cup' for 'the cup's brightness.' Placed as a verb, you write 'the cup sun-and-moons,' actually 'cup sun-and-moon,' or in a weakened thought, 'is like sun,' i.e. shines. 'Sun-and-moon cup' is naturally a bright cup. There is no possible confusion of the real meaning, though a stupid scholar may spend a week trying to decide what 'part of speech' he should use in translating a very simple and direct thought from Chinese to English.

The fact is that almost every written Chinese word is properly just such an underlying word, and yet it is *not* abstract. It is not exclusive of parts of speech, but comprehensive; not something which is neither a noun, verb, nor adjective, but something which is all of them at once and at all times. Usage may incline the full meaning now a little more to one side, now to another, according to the point of view, but through all cases the poet is free to deal with it richly and concretely, as does nature.

In the derivation of nouns from verbs, the Chinese language is forestalled by the Aryan. Almost all the Sanskrit roots, which seem to underlie European languages, are

---

*[A good writer would use 'shine' (i.e. to shine), 'shining', and 'the shine' or 'sheen', possibly thinking of the German '*schöne*' and '*Schönheit*'; but this does not invalidate Professor Fenollosa's contention. E.P.]

primitive verbs, which express characteristic actions of visible nature. The verb must be the primary fact of nature, since motion and change are all that we can recognise in her. In the primitive transitive sentence, such as ' Farmer pounds rice,' the agent and the object are nouns only in so far as they limit a unit of action. ' Farmer ' and ' rice ' are mere hard terms which define the extremes of the pounding. But in themselves, apart from this sentence-function, they are naturally verbs. The farmer is one who tills the ground, and the rice is a plant which grows in a special way. This is indicated in the Chinese characters. And this probably exemplifies the ordinary derivation of nouns from verbs. In all languages, Chinese included, a noun is originally ' that which does something,' that which performs the verbal action. Thus the moon comes from the root *ma,* and means, ' the measurer.' The sun means that which begets.

The derivation of adjectives from the verb need hardly be exemplified. Even with us, today, we can still watch participles passing over into adjectives. In Japanese the adjective is frankly part of the inflection of the verb, a special mood, so that every verb is also an adjective. This brings us close to nature, because everywhere the quality is only a power of action regarded as having an abstract inherence. Green is only a certain rapidity of vibration, hardness a degree of tenseness in cohering. In Chinese the adjective always retains a substratum of verbal meaning. We should try to render this in translation, not be content with some bloodless adjectival abstraction plus ' is.'

Still more interesting are the Chinese ' prepositions ' — they are often post-positions. Prepositions are so important, so pivotal in European speech only because we have weakly yielded up the force of our intransitive verbs. We have to add small supernumerary words to bring back the original power. We still say ' I see a horse,' but with the weak verb ' look ' we have to add the directive particle ' at ' before we can restore the natural transitiveness.*

Prepositions represent a few simple ways in which incomplete verbs complete themselves. Pointing toward nouns as a limit, they bring force to bear upon them. That is to say, they are naturally verbs, of generalised or condensed use. In Aryan languages it is often difficult to trace the verbal origins of simple prepositions. Only in ' *off* ' do we see a fragment of the thought ' to throw off.' In Chinese the preposition is frankly a verb, specially used in a generalised sense. These verbs are often used in their special verbal sense, and it greatly weakens an English translation if they are systematically rendered by colorless prepositions.

Thus in Chinese, by=to cause; to=to fall toward; in =to remain, to dwell; from=to follow; and so on.

Conjunctions are similarly derivative; they usually serve to mediate actions between verbs, and therefore they are necessarily themselves actions. Thus in Chinese, because=to use; and=to be included under one; another form of ' and ' =to be parallel; or=to partake; if=to let one do, to permit. The same is true of a host of other particles, no longer traceable in the Aryan tongues.

Pronouns appear a thorn in our evolution theory, since they have been taken as unanalysable expressions of personality. In Chinese, even they yield up their striking secrets of verbal metaphor. They are a constant source of weakness if colorlessly translated. Take, for example, the five

*[This is a bad example : we can say ' I look a fool '. ' Look ', transitive, now means resemble. The main contention is, however, correct. We tend to abandon specific words like *resemble* and substitute, for them, vague verbs with prepositional directors, or riders. E.P.]

forms of ' I.' There is the sign of a ' spear in the hand '=a
very emphatic I; five and a mouth=a weak and defensive
I, holding off a crowd by speaking; to conceal=a selfish and
private I; self (the cocoon sign) and a mouth=an egoistic I,
one who takes pleasure in his own speaking; the self pre-
sented is used only when one is speaking to one's self.

I trust that this digression concerning parts of speech may
have justified itself. It proves, first, the enormous interest of
the Chinese language in throwing light upon our forgotten
mental processes, and thus furnishes a new chapter in the
philosophy of language. Secondly, it is indispensable for
understanding the poetical raw material which the Chinese
language affords. Poetry differs from prose in the concrete
colors of its diction. It is not enough for it to furnish a
meaning to philosophers. It must appeal to emotions with
the charm of direct impression, flashing through regions
where the intellect can only grope.* Poetry must render
what is said, not what is merely meant. Abstract meaning
gives little vividness, and fullness of imagination gives all.
Chinese poetry demands that we abandon our narrow
grammatical categories, that we follow the original text
with a wealth of concrete verbs.

But this is only the beginning of the matter. So far we
have exhibited the Chinese characters and the Chinese sen-
tence chiefly as vivid shorthand pictures of actions and pro-
cesses in nature. These embody true poetry as far as they
go. Such actions are *seen,* but Chinese would be a poor
language, and Chinese poetry but a narrow art, could they
not go on to represent also what is unseen. The best poetry
deals not only with natural images but with lofty thoughts,
spiritual suggestions and obscure relations. The greater part
of natural truth is hidden in processes too minute for vision

*[Cf. principle of Primary apparition, ' Spirit of Romance '. E.P.]

and in harmonies too large, in vibrations, cohesions and in affinities. The Chinese compass these also, and with great power and beauty.

You will ask, how could the Chinese have built up a great intellectual fabric from mere picture writing? To the ordinary Western mind, which believes that thought is concerned with logical categories and which rather condemns the faculty of direct imagination, this feat seems quite impossible. Yet the Chinese language with its peculiar materials has passed over from the seen to the unseen by exactly the same process which all ancient races employed. This process is metaphor, the use of material images to suggest immaterial relations.*

The whole delicate substance of speech is built upon substrata of metaphor. Abstract terms, pressed by etymology, reveal their ancient roots still embedded in direct action. But the primitive metaphors do not spring from arbitrary *subjective* processes. They are possible only because they follow objective lines of relations in nature herself. Relations are more real and more important than the things which they relate. The forces which produce the branch-angles of an oak lay potent in the acorn. Similar lines of resistance, half-curbing the out-pressing vitalities, govern the branching of rivers and of nations. Thus a nerve, a wire, a roadway, and a clearing-house are only varying channels which communication forces for itself. This is more than analogy, it is identity of structure. Nature furnishes her own clues. Had the world not been full of homologies, sympathies, and identities, thought would have been starved and language chained to the obvious. There would have been no bridge whereby to cross from the minor truth

*[Compare Aristotle's *Poetics*: 'Swift perception of relations, hallmark of genius'. E.P.]

of the seen to the major truth of the unseen. Not more than a few hundred roots out of our large vocabularies could have dealt directly with physical processes. These we can fairly well identify in primitive Sanskrit. They are, almost without exception, vivid verbs. The wealth of European speech grew, following slowly the intricate maze of nature's suggestions and affinities. Metaphor was piled upon metaphor in quasi-geological strata.

Metaphor, the revealer of nature, is the very substance of poetry. The known interprets the obscure, the universe is alive with myth. The beauty and freedom of the observed world furnish a model, and life is pregnant with art. It is a mistake to suppose, with some philosophers of aesthetics, that art and poetry aim to deal with the general and the abstract. This misconception has been foisted upon us by mediaeval logic. Art and poetry deal with the concrete of nature, not with rows of separate ' particulars,' for such rows do not exist. Poetry is finer than prose because it gives us more concrete truth in the same compass of words. Metaphor, its chief device, is at once the substance of nature and of language. Poetry only does consciously* what the primitive races did unconsciously. The chief work of literary men in dealing with language, and of poets especially, lies in feeling back along the ancient lines of advance.† He must do this so that he may keep his words

---

*[*Vide* also an article on ' Vorticism ' in the *Fortnightly Review* for September 1914. ' The language of exploration ' now in my ' Gaudier-Brzeska '. E.P.]

†[I would submit in all humility that this applies in the rendering of ancient texts. The poet, in dealing with his own time, must also see to it that language does not petrify on his hands. He must prepare for new advances along the lines of true metaphor, that is interpretative metaphor, or image, as diametrically opposed to untrue, or ornamental, metaphor. E.P.]

enriched by all their subtle undertones of meaning. The original metaphors stand as a kind of luminous background, giving color and vitality, forcing them closer to the concreteness of natural processes. Shakespeare everywhere teems with examples. For these reasons poetry was the earliest of the world arts; poetry, language and the care of myth grew up together.

I have alleged all this because it enables me to show clearly why I believe that the Chinese written language has not only absorbed the poetic substance of nature and built with it a second work of metaphor, but has, through its very pictorial visibility, been able to retain its original creative poetry with far more vigor and vividness than any phonetic tongue. Let us first see how near it is to the heart of nature in its metaphors. We can watch it passing from the seen to the unseen, as we saw it passing from verb to pronoun. It retains the primitive sap, it is not cut and dried like a walking-stick. We have been told that these people are cold, practical, mechanical, literal, and without a trace of imaginative genius. That is nonsense.

Our ancestors built the accumulations of metaphor into structures of language and into systems of thought. Languages today are thin and cold because we think less and less into them. We are forced, for the sake of quickness and sharpness, to file down each word to its narrowest edge of meaning. Nature would seem to have become less like a paradise and more and more like a factory. We are content to accept the vulgar misuse of the moment.

A late stage of decay is arrested and embalmed in the dictionary.

Only scholars and poets feel painfully back along the thread of our etymologies and piece together our diction, as best they may, from forgotten fragments. This anaemia of modern speech is only too well encouraged by the feeble cohesive force of our phonetic symbols. There is little or nothing in a phonetic word to exhibit the embryonic stages of its growth. It does not bear its metaphor on its face. We forget that personality once meant, not the soul, but the soul's mask. This is the sort of thing one can not possibly forget in using the Chinese symbols.

In this Chinese shows its advantage. Its etymology is constantly visible. It retains the creative impulse and process, visible and at work. After thousands of years the lines of metaphoric advance are still shown, and in many cases actually retained in the meaning. Thus a word, instead of growing gradually poorer and poorer as with us, becomes richer and still more rich from age to age, almost consciously luminous. Its uses in national philosophy and history, in biography and in poetry, throw about it a nimbus of meanings. These centre about the graphic symbol. The memory can hold them and use them. The very soil of Chinese life seems entangled in the roots of its speech. The manifold illustrations which crowd its annals of personal experience, the lines of tendency which converge upon a tragic climax, moral character as the very core of the principle — all these are flashed at once on the mind as reinforcing values with accumulation of meaning which a phonetic language can hardly hope to attain. Their ideographs are like blood-stained battle-flags to an old campaigner. With us, the poet is the only one for whom the accumulated treasures of the race-words are real and active. Poetic language is always vibrant with fold on fold of overtones and with natural affinities, but in Chinese the visibility of the metaphor tends to raise this quality to its intensest power.

I have mentioned the tyranny of mediaeval logic. According to this European logic thought is a kind of brickyard.

It is baked into little hard units or concepts. These are piled in rows according to size and then labeled with words for future use. This use consists in picking out a few bricks, each by its convenient label, and sticking them together into a sort of wall called a sentence by the use either of white mortar for the positive copula ' is,' or of black mortar for the negative copula ' is not.' In this way we produce such admirable propositions as ' A ring-tailed baboon is not a constitutional assembly.'

Let us consider a row of cherry trees. From each of these in turn we proceed to take an ' abstract,' as the phrase is, a certain common lump of qualities which we may express together by the name cherry or cherry-ness. Next we place in a second table several such characteristic concepts: cherry, rose, sunset, iron-rust, flamingo. From these we abstract some further common quality, dilutation or mediocrity, and label it ' red ' or ' redness.' It is evident that this process of abstraction may be carried on indefinitely and with all sorts of material. We may go on for ever building pyramids of attenuated concept until we reach the apex ' being.'

But we have done enough to illustrate the characteristic process. At the base of the pyramid lie *things,* but stunned, as it were. They can never know themselves for things until they pass up and down among the layers of the pyramids. The way of passing up and down the pyramid may be exemplified as follows : We take a concept of lower attenuation, such as ' cherry '; we see that it is contained under one higher, such as ' redness.' Then we are permitted to say in sentence form, ' Cherryness is contained under redness,' or for short, '(The) cherry is red.' If, on the other hand, we do not find our chosen subject under a given predicate we use the black copula and say, for example, '(The) cherry is not liquid.'

From this point we might go on to the theory of the syllogism, but we refrain. It is enough to note that the practised logician finds it convenient to store his mind with long lists of nouns and adjectives, for these are naturally the names of classes. Most text-books on language begin with such lists. The study of verbs is meagre, for in such a system there is only one real working verb, to wit, the quasi-verb ' is.' All other verbs can be transformed into participles and gerunds. For example, ' to run ' practically becomes a case of ' running.' Instead of thinking directly, ' The man runs,' our logician makes two subjective equations, namely : The individual in question is contained under the class ' man '; and the class ' man ' is contained under the class of ' running things.'

The sheer loss and weakness of this method are apparent and flagrant. Even in its own sphere it can not think half of what it wants to think. It has no way of bringing together any two concepts which do not happen to stand one under the other and in the same pyramid.

It is impossible to represent change in this system or any kind of growth.

This is probably why the conception of evolution came so late in Europe. *It could not make way until it was prepared to destroy the inveterate logic of classsification.*

Far worse than this, such logic can not deal with any kind of interaction or with any multiplicity of function. According to it, the function of my muscles is as isolated from the function of my nerves, as from an earthquake in the moon. For it the poor neglected things at the bases of the pyramids are only so many particulars or pawns.

Science fought till she got at the things.

All her work has been done from the base of the pyramids, not from the apex. She has discovered how functions cohere in things. She expresses her results in grouped sentences which embody no nouns or adjectives but verbs of special character. The true formula for thought is: The cherry tree is all that it does. Its correlated verbs compose it. At bottom these verbs are transitive. Such verbs may be almost infinite in number.

In diction and in grammatical form science is utterly opposed to logic. Primitive men who created language agreed with science and not with logic. Logic has abused the language which they left to her mercy.

Poetry agrees with science and not with logic.

The moment we use the copula, the moment we express subjective inclusions, poetry evaporates. The more concretely and vividly we express the interactions of things the better the poetry. We need in poetry thousands of active words, each doing its utmost to show forth the motive and vital forces. We can not exhibit the wealth of nature by mere summation, by the piling of sentences. Poetic thought works by suggestion, crowding maximum meaning into the single phrase pregnant, charged, and luminous from within.

In Chinese character each word accumulated this sort of energy in itself.

Should we pass formally to the study of Chinese poetry, we should warn ourselves against logicianised pitfalls. We should be ware of modern narrow utilitarian meanings ascribed to the words in commercial dictionaries. We should try to preserve the metaphoric overtones. We should be ware of English grammar, its hard parts of speech, and its lazy satisfaction with nouns and adjectives. We should seek and at least bear in mind the verbal undertone of each noun. We should avoid ' is ' and bring in a wealth of neglected English verbs. Most of the existing translations violate all of these rules.

The development of the normal transitive sentence rests upon the fact that one action in nature promotes another; thus the agent and the object are secretly verbs. For example, our sentence, ' Reading promotes writing,' would be expressed in Chinese by three full verbs. Such a form is the equivalent of three expanded clauses and can be drawn out into adjectival, participial, infinitive, relative or conditional members. One of many possible examples is, ' If one reads it teaches him how to write.' Another is, ' One who reads becomes one who writes.' But in the first condensed form a Chinese would write, ' Read promote write.' The dominance of the verb and its power to obliterate all other parts of speech give us the model of terse fine style.

I have seldom seen our rhetoricians dwell on the fact that the great strength of our language lies in its splendid array of transitive verbs, drawn both from Anglo-Saxon and from Latin sources. These give us the most individual characterisations of force. Their power lies in their recognition of nature as a vast storehouse of forces. We do not say in English that things seem, or appear, or eventuate, or even that they are; but that they *do*. Will is the foundation of our speech.* We catch the Demi-urge in the act. I had to discover for myself why Shakespeare's English was so immeasurably superior to all others. I found that it was his persistent, natural, and magnificent use of hundreds of transitive verbs. Rarely will you find an ' is ' in his sentences. ' Is ' weakly lends itself to the uses of our rhythm, in the unaccented syllables; yet he sternly discards it. A study of Shakespeare's verbs should underlie all exercises in style.

We find in poetical Chinese a wealth of transitive verbs, in some way greater even than in the English of Shakes-

*[Compare Dante's definition of ' rectitudo ' as the direction of the will.]

peare. This springs from their power of combining several pictorial elements in a single character. We have in English no verb for what two things, say the sun and moon, both do together. Prefixes and affixes merely direct and qualify. In Chinese the verb can be more minutely qualified. We find a hundred variants clustering about a single idea. Thus ' to sail a boat for purposes of pleasure ' would be an entirely different verb from ' to sail for purposes of commerce.' Dozens of Chinese verbs express various shades of grieving, yet in English translations they are usually reduced to one mediocrity. Many of them can be expressed only by periphrasis, but what right has the translator to neglect the overtones? There are subtle shadings. We should strain our resources in English.

It is true that the pictorial clue of many Chinese ideographs can not now be traced, and even Chinese lexicographers admit that combinations frequently contribute only a phonetic value. But I find it incredible that any such minute subdivision of the idea could have ever existed alone as abstract sound without the concrete character. It contradicts the law of evolution. Complex ideas arise only gradually, as the power of holding them together arises. The paucity of Chinese sound could not so hold them. Neither is it conceivable that the whole list was made at once, as commercial codes of cipher are compiled. Foreign words sometimes recalled Chinese ideograms associated with vaguely similar sound? Therefore we must believe that the phonetic theory is in large part unsound? The metaphor once existed in many cases where we can not now trace it. Many of our own etymologies have been lost. It is futile to take the ignorance of the Han dynasty for omniscience.*

*[Professor Fenollosa is borne out by chance evidence. Gaudier-Brzeska sat in my room before he went off to war. He was able to

It is not true, as Legge said, that the original picture charac-
ters could never have gone far in building up abstract
thought. This is a vital mistake. We have seen that our own
languages have all sprung from a few hundred vivid phone-
tic verbs by figurative derivation. A fabric more vast could
have been built up in Chinese by metaphorical composition.
No attenuated idea exists which it might not have reached
more vividly and more permanently than we could have
been expected to reach with phonetic roots. Such a pictorial
method, whether the Chinese exemplified it or not, would
be the ideal language of the world.

Still, is it not enough to show that Chinese poetry gets
back near to the processes of nature by means of its vivid
figure, its wealth of such figure? If we attempt to follow it
in English we must use words highly charged, words whose
vital suggestion shall interplay as nature interplays. Sen-
tences must be like the mingling of the fringes of feathered
banners, or as the colors of many flowers blended into the
single sheen of a meadow.

The poet can never see too much or feel too much. His

read the Chinese radicals and many compound signs almost at pleasure.
He was used to consider all life and nature in the terms of planes and
of bounding lines. Nevertheless he had spent only a fortnight in the
museum studying the Chinese characters. He was amazed at the
stupidity of lexicographers who could not, for all their learning discern
the pictorial values which were to him perfectly obvious and apparent.
A few weeks later Edmond Dulac, who is of a totally different tradi-
tion, sat here, giving an impromptu panegyric on the elements of
Chinese art, on the units of composition, drawn from the written
characters. He did not use Professor Fenollosa's own words — he said
'bamboo' instead of 'rice'. He said the essence of the bamboo is in
a certain way it grows; they have this in their sign for bamboo, all
designs of bamboo proceed from it. Then he went on rather to dis-
parage vorticism, on the grounds that it could not hope to do for the
Occident, in one lifetime, what had required centuries of development
in China. E.P.]

metaphors are only ways of getting rid of the dead white plaster of the copula. He resolves its indifference into a thousand tints of verb. His figures flood things with jets of various light, like the sudden up-blaze of fountains. The prehistoric poets who created language discovered the whole harmonious framework of nature, they sang out her processes in their hymns. And this diffused poetry which they created, Shakespeare has condensed into a more tangible substance. Thus in all poetry a word is like a sun, with its corona and chromosphere; words crowd upon words, and enwrap each other in their luminous envelopes until sentences become clear, continuous light-bands.

Now we are in condition to appreciate the full splendor of certain lines of Chinese verse. Poetry surpasses prose especially in that the poet selects for juxtaposition those words whose overtones blend into a delicate and lucid harmony. All arts follow the same law; refined harmony lies in the delicate balance of overtones. In music the whole possibility and theory of harmony are based on the overtones. In this sense poetry seems a more difficult art.

How shall we determine the metaphorical overtones of neighbouring words? We can avoid flagrant breaches like mixed metaphor. We can find the concord or harmonising at its intensest, as in Romeo's speech over the dead Juliet.

Here also the Chinese ideography has its advantage, in even a simple line; for example, ' The sun rises in the east.'

The overtones vibrate against the eye. The wealth of composition in characters makes possible a choice of words in which a single dominant overtone colors every plane of meaning. That is perhaps the most conspicuous quality of Chinese poetry. Let us examine our line.

33

Sun   Rises   (in the)   East

The sun, the shining, on one side, on the other the sign of
the east, which is the sun entangled in the branches of a
tree. And in the middle sign, the verb ' rise,' we have
further homology; the sun is above the horizon, but beyond
that the single upright line is like the growing trunk-line of
the tree sign. This is but a beginning, but it points a way
to the method, and to the method of intelligent reading.

TERMINAL NOTE. E.P., 1935. Whatever a few of us learned from
Fenollosa twenty years ago, the whole Occident is still in crass ignor-
ance of the Chinese art of verbal sonority. I now doubt if it was
inferior to the Greek. Our poets being slovenly, ignorant of music,
and earless, it is useless to blame professors for squalor.

雪　晴　如　耀　月

晃　照　似　花　梅

轉　鏡　金　憐　可

馨　芳　玉　上　庭

PLATE 1

35

[Fenollosa left the notes unfinished; I am proceeding in ignorance and by conjecture. The primitive pictures were "squared" at a certain time. E.P.]

MOON	RAYS	LIKE	PURE	SNOW
sun disc with the moon's horns	bright + feathers flying. Bright, *vide* note on p. 42. Upper right, abbreviated picture of wings; lower, bird=to fly. Both F. and Morrison note that it is short tailed bird	woman mouth	sun + azure sky. Sky possibly containing tent idea. Author has dodged a "pure" containing 'sun' + broom	rain + broom. cloud roof or cloth over falling drops. Sweeping motion of snow; broom-like appearance of snow

PLUM	FLOWERS	RESEMBLE	BRIGHT	STARS
tree + crooked female breast	man + spoon under plants abbreviation, probably actual representation of blossoms. Flowers at height of man's head. Two forms of character in F.'s two copies	man + try = does what it can toward	sun + knife mouth fire	sun bright. Bright here going to origin: fire over moving legs of a man

CAN	ADMIRE	GOLD	DISC	TURN
mouth hook. I suppose it might even be fish-pole or sheltered corner	(*be in love with*) fire. heart + girl + descending through two	Present form resembles king and gem; but archaic might be balance and melting-pots	to erect. gold + sun legs (running)	carriage + carriage. tenth of cubit. (?) Bent knuckle or bent object revolving round pivot

GARDEN	HIGH ABOVE	JEWEL	WEEDS	FRAGRANT
to blend + pace, in midst of court		king and dot. *Note:* Plain man + dot = dog	plants cover knife. I.e. growing things that must be destroyed	Specifically given in Morrison as fragrance from a distance. M. and F. seem to differ as to significance of sun under growing tree (cause of fragrance)

NOTE ON PLATE 1

The component 'bright' in the second ideogram is resolvable into fire above a man (walking). The picture is abbreviated to the light and the moving legs. I should say it might have started as the sun god moving below the horizon, at any rate it is the upper part of the fire sign. This also applies in line 2, fifth ideogram, where the legs are clearer. The rain sign (developed in snow sign) might suggest the cloths of heaven, tent roof.

The large base of the last composite sign (Fragrant) Morrison considers as merely a buried sun.

Starting at top left, we have scholar over something like a corpse (a sign I find only in compounds: (?) a wounded corpse). This pair alone form 'a vulgar form of sign,' or an abbreviation of the full sign for 'voice, notes of music, sound, any noise,' also abbreviation for noise of a blow; to the right of it 'weapons like spears or flails'; this compound=enemy; and our total, sun under tree under enemy.

PARAPHRASE

The moon's snow falls on the plum tree;
Its boughs are full of bright stars.
We can admire the bright turning disc;
The garden high above there, casts its pearls to our weeds.

Loss in interaction being apparent on study of the ideograms, their inter-relation, and the repetition or echo of components, not only those used but those suggested or avoided.

A poem of moonlight; the sun element is contained five times: once in three lines, and twice in the second.

You have not understood the poem until you have seen the tremendous antithesis from the first line to the last; from the first character, diagonal, to the last tremendous affirmative, sun under tree under enemies.

Ideograms Line 1, No. 2; Line 2, No. 2; and Line 4, No. 5 — almost every alternate sign — are such compendiums as should make clear to us the estimate courtiers put upon single characters written by the old Empress Dowager, after the age-old custom. Line 3, No. 2, Fenollosa had translated admire, then changed to love; I have taken back to admire, for the sake of Latin *ad-miror* and to absorb some of Morrison's 'implement used to reflect,' though I do not imagine this will reach many readers.

When you have comprehended the visual significance, you will not have finished. There is still the other dimension. We will remain bestially ignorant of Chinese poetry so long as we insist on reading and *speaking* their short words instead of taking time to sing them with observance of the sequence of vowels.

If Chinese 'tone' is a forbidden district, an incomprehensible mystery, vowel *leadings* exist for anyone who can LISTEN.

If our universities had been worth half a peck of horse-dung, something would have been done during the last quarter of a century to carry on Fenollosa's work. Millions have been spent in stultifying education. There is no reason, apart from usury and the hatred of letters, for keeping at least a few hundred poems and the Ta Hio out of bilingual edition, such as I am here giving for this quatrain. The infamy of the present monetary system does not stop with the malnutrition of the masses; it extends upward into every cranny of the intellectual life, even where cowards think themselves safest, and though men of low vitality feel sure boredom can never kill.

The state of Chinese studies in the Occident is revoltingly squalid, and one has to read Frobenius in his own language? Because English and American professors are moles.

Confucius' statement, ' A man's character is apparent in every brush-stroke ': the high value set by the Chinese on calligraphy is appreciable when you think that if the writer does not do his ideogram well, the suggestion of the picture does not carry. If he does not know the meaning of the elements, his ignorance leaks through every ink-mark.

石　伙　舟
男　迥　溿
古　灰　舳
伏　旦　訑
東　担　峯
春　王　峰

PLATE 2

NOTE ON PLATE 2

COLUMN 1

1. A boat (? scow), probably people riding in the boat.
2. Water by boat=ripple.
3. Boat+, I should think, actual picture of the rudder. Morrison gives this second element as development of field sign, something just adjacent to, or coming out of, field. (The field supposed to represent grain in orderly rows.) With primitive sign, the shoot coming from field would contain idea of causation. The element means ' by,' ' from '; the whole sign=rudder.
4. Speech+grass growing with difficulty (i.e. twisted root and obstacle above it)=appearance of speaking in a confused manner.
5. To follow, over branching horns (together meaning to fight like two bulls), above this a mountain=peak of a hill going perpendicular toward heaven and ending in a point.
6. Morrison gives an ideogram with the mountain sign a little lower, and says it is same as the preceding, but possibly misses the point. F. gives this ideogram with the mountain in odd position as=a peak that clashes with heaven.

COLUMN 2

1. Man+fire=messmate.
2. Water+revolve within a circle=eddy.
3. Hand+fire=fire that can be taken in the hand=cinder, ashes.
4. Sun above line of horizon=dawn.
5. Earth (sign not very well drawn — left lower stroke should be at bottom)+the foregoing=level plain, wide horizon.
6. One who binds three planes: heaven, earth and man=ruler, to rule.

COLUMN 3

1. A lump of matter under a cliff (in primitive sign the lump was further removed)=a detached stone.
2. Rice-field over struggle=MALE.
3. Ten over mouth=old, what has come down through ten generations, ten mouths of tradition.
4. Man+dog (dot beside man)=dog lying at man's feet or crawling to man's feet; hence, to lie down.
5. Sun rising, showing through tree's branches=the east.
6. Spring season, hilarity, wantonness. Looks like sun under man and tree, but the early forms all show sun under growing branches, profuse branches and grass.

SECTION 1   SECTION 2

PLATE 3

NOTE ON PLATE 3

Compare these last inventions to the twenty-two pages double column of Morrison devoted to HORSE.

Self-effacement, to put away evil,
          earth over self (crooked elbow (?)).

Water + the foregoing, water level, universal usage,
          law (Buddhist term).

Self-effacement over sacrificial dish = many persons uniting eagerly
          together = to unite.

Idem, whom closed door includes = family.

SECTION 2

Man and word, man standing by his word, man of his word, truth,
          sincere, unwavering.

The word sign is radical supposedly from combination of tongue and
          above : ? mouth with tongue coming out it.

凡 主 厶

八 出 言

一 屯 支

PLATE 4

NOTE ON PLATE 4

COLUMN 1

Self, crooked. Ancient form is loop-like, but the form now used suggests bent elbow, mighty biceps idea familiar in Armstrong and Strongi'th'arm insignia. The use of this sign for emphasis is certainly not discordant with this suggestion, which can at any rate serve as mnemonic.

Mouth with 'two words and flame emerging' (acc. F.)=to speak, words.

Branch, radical.

COLUMN 2

Flame in midst of lamp, extended to mean lord, master, to govern.

(?) Morrison's form slightly different, plant growing but not detached from earth; the radical is now bud.

Plant with twisted root=to grow with difficulty; note also obstacle top left.

COLUMN 3

Table, bench or stool with dot under it=every, common, vulgar. I suppose 'any old thing,' what one throws under table.

To be divided.

To begin, to appear as one. The significance of these two radimentary signs as given by F. is extremely important.

The student who hurries over the simple radicals or fundamentals will lose a great deal of time; he will also find much greater difficulty in remembering the combinations of such fundamentals which serve as radicals in the dictionary.

德人無累

大鈞播物

PLATE 5

NOTE ON PLATE 5

TOP LINE

1. VIRTUE or virtu, to pace (two men or man in two places; or seen near and at little distance)+heart under sacrificial dish under ten.

2. MAN (radical).

3. NOT POSSESSING. Morrison says: 'Etymology not clear. It is certainly fire under what looks like a fence, but primitive sign does not look like fire but like *bird*. At wild guess I should say primitive sign looks like 'birdie has flown ' (off with the branch). F. gives it as ' lost in a forest.'

4. This sign is clearly a FIELD over SILK THREAD (though I can not find it in Morrison), indicating that the whole source of the man's existence is balanced on next to nothingness.
    M. gives silk beside field=petty, trifling, attenuated, subtle.

SECOND LINE

1. GREAT (man with ample arms).

2. GOLD+equally blended. (The gold sign=also metal, thence the metal). (M. gives Keun, similar but not identical sign, weight of 90 catties. His dots are a little different.)

3. A measure+divide (radical 165, claws) over field.
4. A measure+banner (rally banner).

I have not found the last three characters in Morrison, but one can make sense from the radicals contained in them thus:

Virtue, man not possessing=a man without virtue; all his basis (his source of being and action) is balanced on a weak silk thread; the entire man has the even blending of metals (at his command) and knoweth measure in dividing and in bringing together. Knows how and when to divide a field with justice, and when (and in what degree) to unite (to rally men, concentrate them for action).

CITY LIGHTS PUBLICATIONS

Angulo de, Jaime. INDIANS IN OVERALLS
Angulo de, J.and G. de Angulo. JAIME IN TAOS
Artaud, Antonin. ARTAUD ANTHOLOGY
Bataille, Georges. EROTISM: Death and Sensuality
Bataille, Georges. STORY OF THE EYE
Bataille, Georges. THE TEARS OF EROS
Baudelaire, Charles. INTIMATE JOURNALS
Baudelaire, Charles. TWENTY PROSE POEMS
Bowles, Paul. A HUNDRED CAMELS IN THE COURTYARD
Bukowski, Charles. THE MOST BEAUTIFUL WOMAN IN TOWN
Bukowski, Charles. NOTES OF A DIRTY OLD MAN
Bukowski, Charles. TALES OF ORDINARY MADNESS
Burroughs, William S. THE BURROUGHS FILE
Burroughs, William S. THE YAGE LETTERS
Cardenal, Ernesto. FROM NICARAGUA WITH LOVE
Cassady, Neal. THE FIRST THIRD
Choukri, Mohamed. FOR BREAD ALONE
CITY LIGHTS REVIEW #1: Politics and Poetry issue
CITY LIGHTS REVIEW #2: Forum AIDS and the Arts issue
CITY LIGHTS REVIEW #3: Media and Propaganda issue
CITY LIGHTS REVIEW #4: Ecology / Eastern Europe issue
Cocteau, Jean. THE WHITE BOOK (LE LIVRE BLANC)
Codrescu, Andrei, ed. EXQUISITE CORPSE READER
Cornford, Adam. ANIMATIONS
David-Neel, Alexandra. SECRET ORAL TEACHINGS IN
    TIBETAN BUDDHIST SECTS
Deleuze, Gilles. SPINOZA: PRACTICAL PHILOSOPHY
Dick, Leslie. WITHOUT FALLING
di Prima, Diane. PIECES OF A SONG: Selected Poems
Doolittle, Hilda (H.D.). NOTES ON THOUGHT & VISION
Ducornet, Rikki. ENTERING FIRE
Duras, Marguerite. DURAS BY DURAS
Eidus, Janice. VITO LOVES GERALDINE
Eberhardt, Isabelle. THE OBLIVION SEEKERS
Ferlinghetti, Lawrence. PICTURES OF THE GONE WORLD